The Self as Constellation

poems by Jeanine Hathaway

2001 Winner, Vassar Miller Prize in Poetry
Madeline DeFrees, Judge

University of North Texas Press
Denton, Texas

10 9 8 7 6 5 4 3 2 1

Permissions:
University of North Texas Press
P.O. Box 311336
Denton, TX 76203-1336

The paper used in this book meets the minimum requirements of the American
National Standard for Permanence of Paper for Printed Library Materials,
z39.48.1984. Binding materials have been chosen for durability.

Library of Congress Cataloging-in-Publication Data

Hathaway, Jeanine.
The self as constellation : poems / by Jeanine Hathaway.
p.   cm.
ISBN 1-57441-144-6 (pbk. : alk. paper)
I. Title.
PS3558.A746 S45 2002
811'.54—dc21   2001006779

Page 70 represents an extension of the copyright page.

Design by Angela Schmitt
The enamel on the cover is by Linda Gebert

THE SELF AS CONSTELLATION

CONTENTS

Stars, Fixed and Variable

The Hermit Woman

For my daughter, Margaret, who continues to fill me with new life

Stars, Fixed and Variable

DEATH AND TRACKING

A trapper's trick:
God howls in her
his confusion of rhythms,
his urgent path. Alert,
she slips into his vein,
follows the river, crossing,
re-crossing, the way a lover
ignores her own limits,
back to the frozen source
far inside where she is
a wolf eating God's bloody snow,
licking up what might have been
herself. Elusive as dusk, purple;
she turns: good hunter,
difficult prey.

THE SELF AS CONSTELLATION

The other woman in me loves the unlit
clouds roiling under the face
of the moon like childhood fears,
the hurry and snap of trees, branches
scratching at our screens, noises
let out of their harness at night.

I settle indoors and build
a fire, its rush and crackle
contained small on the other side
of the screen. I pull out a thick
novel, an orderly world, everything
left in, left out for human reasons.
I untie my hair.

The other woman dresses heavy,
warm, rustles around beyond my book
gathering equipment—flashlight,
extra hat, sleeping bag, brandied fruit.
She leaves her glasses on my dresser.

We create our own balance and tension
and four-legged gait. Neither of us
knows what the other sees as
we look out through the same eyes.

What she can expect tomorrow: me
asleep near my book and cold fire.
And I: her, rising early, coming in
with the milk and the morning star.

PREPARING THE WAY

It is advent, says the priest, *the time to expect*
what cannot possibly be. Think of Mary. . .
A woman in the back of church shudders
recalling her own pregnancy, her guilty ambivalence,
anticipation heavy from the outset with sore breasts

and months of soda crackers and white lips,
unable to brush her teeth without gagging.
The thickening belly and need for naps, the
preoccupation, tired, wanting to be left alone,
unaccountable, disembodied; people saying

she certainly had the glow and she seeing the cow
in the mirror, the bloat that used to be her flat
and private body that gave her definition, that
gave her her mind; and all that resenting and anxiety,
wishing she knew who it was and whether or not

it was all there all right swimming, smiling,
kicking up an empire under her ribs. *Expect*
what cannot possibly be: a healthy daughter
who can feed herself, change herself, kiss good-
night and awake in twelve hours precocious,

articulate. *Think of Mary* who gave birth on her
due date with angels and stars; the woman's baby
born two weeks late, coaxed out with gloves and IVs,
wearing a black cap of a birthmark over the back
of her head and the pediatricians and dermatologists

and plastic surgeons looking at each other, saying,
Hmm. Watch it for growths—prone to cancer—sometimes
a growth means it's too late. And the woman leaking
and draining suspects this wild thing, pink and black,
milking her thinking: *this is advent.*

POEM FOR CHRISTMAS

The presence of God With Us like some
squalling little double-cross: guilt.
I want no dutifully eating suitcase
relations, no chorus washed in lamplight
cooing. Against expectations giddy
with ribbon and wrap, I do not choose
the baby. I will wait for the man,
will take him alone, treacherous, alive
on the edge of a desert, where he offers
his ragged salvation with eyes half closed
to anything wild or in heat.

LOOKING BOTH WAYS

As a nun I gave my twenties to God
and assumed the character of baptism
unmistakably inside out which is to say
on the bell sleeve of that wedding white
habit which I still wear in dreams
I can't help but remember.

*

Like the youngest child
who shares her bread in the forest
and so receives a token, a means
to be invisible, to stay awake,
to save herself, I was given
a daughter with a black birthmark
like the shadow of a hand poised
for a long and violent blessing.

WORLD WITHOUT END

The woman who lived here before us
died in childbirth. She comes back
every night, suitcase in hand, looking
for her husband, wanting to wake him,
saying it's time. It's time now.
He is not here anymore. She knows that.
But she is, repeating the final scenes
until she gets them right and can return
home, the great watery world inside her
delivered small and dry.

Rubbing the side of her belly, she moves
through the garden toward the beach,
walks among restive animals, tough grass,
looking for her husband. She is
so pale and big, awkward with the suitcase.
She moves to the lake, waves washing
the sand where she walks. She drops
to her knees, rolls down on her side.
Every night she makes no cry,
no sound at all at the water's edge.

LIKE A JAGUAR

What falls from the tallest growth—
wretched petals, bark, dead bees—
sifts down the jungle's moist pleasures,
the occasional thump of dropped fruit.
In such silence the tumid powers gather,
condense, and move in a new economy
of pelage, sinew, and bone.

Under the canopied forest still
toward you I am drawn through pounding
heat and dread. You are my chance
for loss: long, tawny,
the darkness wet on a victim's throat.
I cannot catch my breath.

On the branch overhanging the river
you stretch, lean and deadly,
your weight rising like light
serene as a predator's dream, the blood
long licked from your paws.
Hunger flicks your tongue as you survey
the thick intercourse of vine and brush,
the shadows you know simply as
—*yawn*—the dimensions of flesh.

METHODS OF ORGANIZATION

In dreamy magazines couples claim one another,
page after page, lingering over distant travel,
sterling and crystal, romantic with berries in heavy
cream, plush towels of remarkable colors draped
over white wicker chairs, and a sense of music
in the open windows.

I felt that urge for clarity, for proclamation,
for a moment's respite, so I looked for you whose
image I knew would rise from a crowded dream,
from a taste for salt, from a note I always
come back to in my secret humming. And there
you were, steady, at home.

Remember the first sign of spring, when the ice
broke up in brilliant reports and great chunks
of it angled down the beach in bell blue chaos?
Since then, seasons have rolled over themselves
like water: swelling, subsiding, swelling again
in startling, clear vitality.

THE LEFT HAND IS COMPLEMENT

Praise to my elders who are my left hand.
My awkward hinge, my elders-hand, the hand
that holds the wallet while the quick one
spends, the hand that hugs the bowl
as the adept stirs the dough, the hand
at the end of the bat for stable opposition.
The hand that wears the ring, my elders,
that says until death, that says
I do (I did); the ring I don't wear any more,
that says this hand has a chance at wisdom
if not dexterity. The hand that, when I am
seated at God's right, will be closest,
will brush against the hand of God
as we pass around desserts.

AMONG THE VERY YOUNG AT ART

The girls have dressed older than they are,
promised decorum, made themselves up
to be part of the show. Without brothers
each searches the hall for her Hansel,
his trousers bulging with safe white stones.

Here's opera to showcase: cannibalism
(bowdlerized kids become cookies,
not steak and kidney pie);
parents crazed by the broom market slump;
how witch burning still wins applause.

Hansel and Gretel. No promised Prince Charming,
no happy forever. They'd still to grow up,
to learn how age will ice even those
who have lived in gingerbread houses,
how sweet crust can turn to cinnamon ash.

The girls, instantly Gretels, are just savvy enough
to lose their own wits and way. May they
warm to a brotherly prompt, but understand
at every stage, something is always cooking.

SINISTER

My daughter reins in her mount, Aristera,
a Greek word for left-handed, root
of aristocracy. This girl's a lefty
polished with lessons: French, piano, dressage.
She's young and I ask myself, shaking my head,
You old romantic, what are you doing?
Marking this tabula rasa to live
in a world that doesn't exist or at best only
once in a while? Like the full moon
or a whole-hearted love or a garden post-harvest
that keeps on producing. What I'm preparing her for
is this world, the panache and pleasure of gross
excess, the frowned upon forms of the familiar.

Think of the dangers of music: babies
conceived to a hard rock beat or mobs
gone blond, frothy with Wagner. Think of the dangers
of horses: being kicked or thrown or seduced
in the dung-slick mythical hay. And the dangers
of language: the power to be flagrantly accurate
in two honey gold tongues. What does this have to do
with being left-handed? Only its other classical root.

SARAH'S ADVICE TO THE LATER CHILDREN

When the climb is finished
and you roll over,
throat exposed, say

there is no ram in the bush?
No angel to stay the knife
and dust you off? What is there

then to stop you from some gesture
of what you must call biblical proportion,
but a fatal lack of practice?

IN RANDOM FIELDS OF IMPULSE AND REPOSE

A man moves toward himself as old,
as his own ancestor: hunting and hunted
though never feeling foreign, his boundaries
set by smell or height, cold or density,
water or none, as though earth herself
had said, "Stop. You are too far from your
own home." And so he stepped back, read
the stars or birds, bargained with some
offering—brother, lamb, jug, weapon—
and stayed just there, at the edge
of the earth's command preferring that
tremor caused by strategic defiance
to the simpler continuity of return.

A man moves toward himself as he will
always return to the man before, the man
inside himself who is for thousands of years
making the bread, lighting the cave,
wearing well. He will call this man
something else, another sex or race, even
a place in a dream. But, he is just
himself returning, carrying his flute and
shovel across the breast of earth and her
ragged history, home.

AFTER SEPARATION

He is wanting the woman whose breath
curled in the cave of his ear like a child
asleep under the night's heart, certain
of its rush of blood and stars
and wintry birds wheeling south
to warmer, wetter times.

> Barley expanding thickens the soup,
> raises the carrots up from the bottom.
> The kitchen windows sweat and run.
> A round rye loaf cools on the rack.
> But the cups on her table are upside down
> and in her mouth is a traveller's coin.

Unaccustomed to filling himself with
himself, he is wanting her weariness—
come from bearing their world
green and forgiven in the cradle
of her arms—and is wanting those arms
to fold like wings again over his back.

AFTER ANOTHER DEATH

Home is where the heat is.
Pull up to that potbelly stove,
see the flame rake into whips, grins,
its energy assumed by subtle calisthenics,
the thermodynamics of family
whose second law is loss.
We sneak an alien look, prepared to flee
even as we huddle, palms flat to the fire,
a gesture that looks like
(as if we could) "stop."

ECLIPSE

One sleepy eye open
toward your side of the bed
I am nearly awake to that
empty spot growing
round as an oracle: round
as the early embrace that paced
my heartbeat to yours; round
as the bond to the branch
the stem breaks
when the leaf knows
past tremble and flight
the comfort of earth,
that earth can be
its only choice.

The air hangs still
over your side,
the curtain flawless,
the window open
to surprise
at this midmorning place
in our orbit: the moon inching
her way toward the sun
in steady proclamation:

love, the power of nothing is final.

MISPERCEPTIONS

Pigeon-breasted women gather at the lavoir.
Peasants bumped up to middle class, they do own washers,
electric boxes nuclear-powered,
they let agitate and wring, then remove the unrinsed load.
Pinchpenny virtue: Save the sous.
On wagons, shoulder poles, heads, they bear
baskets of soapy clothes to rinse for free
in the river's ancient, walled washplace.

Their husbands jeer.
Why did we buy you machines? So
your calves will pop rivers, purple damned
calves, ankles thick as your grandmothers'?
Pagh! They go back to their boules,
to their grousing, to one another.

The women gossip; faster than bugs
their words swarm over cold black water,
rise; white suds thin, disappear
in current swirls. Clean, they are soon
so clean nothing is left to say, not *squeak*.
The lavoir mirrors lines of pinned up
clothes—the lavable life angles into letters:
the V of stiff trousers, the double O bras,
the socks' repetition of L, L, L.
Substantial as the need to get these hung,
the women's speech together was their way
into silence. Their talk was a chant, a curious
liturgy, high courting, sentence, ablution.

What lingers? A confusion of drones
that cling to the lavender scent of detergent,
the widow's breezy flowered sheets.

FOR THE RECENTLY SINGLE, A DATE MEANS

to be chosen, the one among the many. This woman
knows her date's track record, as they say.
He's made his way around her circle of friends.
How they caution her now,
though she's told not a one.
What's a dinner?
She keeps her own counsel, checks
options again for an outfit
that won't remind him of them.
Spirited jodhpurs leap off the shelf.

A date—she lines up the hangers—
is not even a second date. It's a word
to mark one day at a time. The same
word for a sweet fruit, expensive,
exotic, and sticky. She fingers
her dark rose and green silks, smooths
the rumpled, rejected. Her friends
appear like jockeys each alert at her gate.

WOMAN NAMED FOR HER DEAD MOTHER

The woman's name releases her
like water into tidal water
so the name itself might sigh,
might breathe up kelp,
bellywhite fish and sponges,
a chaos she must live on,
never claiming her own
the name of excess.

Near dawn her enormous mother
pulls in nets, sorts, orders
as the dead closely named always do—
the pooled future, syllable
by concentric syllable.

THE SELF AS LINEAR WITH A BELL AT THE END

When the man dies
his name moves in
(with his glasses
and shotgun, warm
hat with flaps,
and a photo of
himself and a young
woman laughing)
behind the eye
of his oldest son.

When the woman dies
her name contracts
round as a lozenge
at the back of her
tongue so at the brash
and unannounced moment
that follows
the moment of death
in her surprised delight
she swallows it
like a baby.

RECONNAISSANCE

Before dawn, before the first
hushed light causes her children
to stir, the woman across the street
rises, every morning, extending
her life backwards into night
as a fish sated at the surface
will dive deeper and darker
until even sight is a memory
floating off.

She is alert now, aware of
herself as out of proportion,
mirrored through water;
expansive, most reflective
and faithful, and still
surrounded, governed
by the immense heartbeat
of her own atmosphere,
the unsettling grace of morning
and her cold feet.

WHEN THE BOUGH BREAKS

One night before a Sunday my brother and I
tore up and burned our mother's Latin missal
because we said it was out of date. Oh tyranny
of guilt, moroccan bound. How do we do it?
Even in song—tyrannous Wagner. Sousa. All
anthems and marches, yes, include the wedding march.
All music heavy on drums, music that mimes
the pulse. Music is tyranny. Color is tyranny.
How many times do the buyer's eyes blink
before red packaging or blue? Is it tyranny
when something is appropriate? Good manners?
The tyranny of please and thank you.
The tyranny of magic words. The tyranny of clothes
that match, the wearer's expectations.
The tyranny of hair: long, short, gray, red, shave
or let grow, the tuft at the crotch of the swimsuit.
The tyranny of housepaint and yardwork,
of bagworms, of spring fever. Of teenagers
parking in front of the house. Of door-to-door
solicitors—Fuller Brush; Trim your hedge, Ma'am?
Candybars or candles for the Junior Hi Band?
Jehovah God knows in multiple forms. Tyrannosaurus
rex: lumbering machismo, the only dinosaur's name
everyone remembers. The tyranny of haste and weight,
the heft of breast and hip, the shapelessness of toes.
The tyranny of interruption—wrong number, right
number, kids who want bailing out of nightmares,
boredom, wreckage. The tyranny of Great Books,
a rich meal eaten late. The tyranny of consequence.
The tyranny of pattern, car route, wardrobe.
The tyranny of many ignoring the few, of the few
disliking the one. Of the one desiring the one,
other. The prodigal tyranny of passion. Of desire
that does not end with having, the tyranny of having,
perfection.

SOMETIMES THE COMING OF BABIES

She wanders onto the balcony
not disturbing the infant asleep
pumping at last his own fatal
blood, a confusion of orchids
and milk. She watches the storks'
black flight feathers, calligraphy
or outlines of white words.
They scatter their clack and hiss—
seven sounds for eating shape seven
for letting go, seven times that
for the tension in eggshell, air,
and wing. For consequence
they make no sound but hop off
gawky from roof to roof bringing
where they nest, some say, good luck.

AN URBAN COSMOLOGY

What's a pastime, what's a city,
what's a heaven for?

Mother and daughter build a city
medieval, posterboard kit; color
the houses, thatch and trees, crenelated
towered wall with scented felt-tipped pens.
Their thirteenth century Normans smell
not like cheese, wet wool, or dog,
but tangerine, coffee, chocolate—
scents unknown for centuries. Polychronic
wizardry! Innocent as sherbet, pens
color prelapsarian life. Who lives here?
What settles in such fragrance?
Does Eden need a wall? Can one be cast
from a boundless place? The builders decide
it wasn't pride that prompted our parents' fall.
Circumference would do, still does to us all.

DIFFERENCE IN AGES

The mother's name flares through language,
a verb unconsumable; a mare dark, fluid,
slick as sex; or through the deck a knife
pointed home.

The daughter's trots forty miles a night
down the participial left, keeping it
fluent, cursing enclosure all the while
moving toward water, its vaporous edge.

FIDO

Disloyal I am, finally un-fido, unfit
American Mom: I don't like dogs.
They stay too long like infants.

Rilke may have seen the folly of mortality in their sad
sympathetic eyes, himself grown richer then, more daring.
Perhaps he had someone to clean up, feed, and walk
his inspiration. Perhaps he was so much himself
a pup, a darling, he skirted what I faced:
dog breath whining, *Look at me—hey! look at me!*

I might've put up longer for the sake of an example:
how to take to the lavish bounds of appetite.
I might've put up for my only child's wish.

But now my butter is free of hair. My hands
unpetting rest in my lap. The noses in my house
are warm and dry. Without interruption I wander
dreamy and grand through my own domain,
the city-peopled side of the Peaceable Kingdom.

THE TURNING POINT

I watch my daughter at her dressage lesson.
Technique and confidence override
metaphor. And I, separate observer,
cannot ever know how
such a brave, slim beauty
will one day assume control, take up
the reins in her quiet hands and ride
through field and forest, dark water and city.
How a girl outgrows the high fence
of a sandy, soft arena, outgrows the fear
of open space and its thousand ways
she and that horse could go.

How one afternoon when the wind riffles through
my hair, thoughts aloft and balmy,
my maternal arms resting heavy on the gates—
that will be the afternoon she decides to open them
and asks me to step back to safety.
There, I am brought up to the point
of so many lessons. What can I do but nod
in recognition of all that might be sent sprawling?
What can I do but swing wide those gates,
walk back to the barn for a mount of my own?

MERCY AS THE CONSTANT

Near his wife before the fire
a man reads a clever tale.
He laughs, explaining why he laughs.
She pokes the fire, thinks of writing
to their children, and wants to remind him,
dear, cleverness is not all, and she does not
say she found his student's letters
in a confidential file in his study.

A writer, he has tried to cushion those
letters in literary terms: setting, plot,
characters: Victorian, romance, December
and May (well, July and October) since
they live a thousand miles apart
collaborating on this story. The preface
took years of professional distance,
reams now reviewed in soft humor
for their touching revelations.

And so once a week each cloisters the Daily
Self and allows an Other to emerge, in candles
and wine and violin solos—to undress
slowly stretching before the judgment
of the other character, to join passions
and furies and linger for an airy moment
beyond the sweet weight of doubt—and
to lie still, page against page, at the end
of the letter, exhausted and inarticulate.

What is it to receive such letters? To play
out a life inside the life in the mirror
with someone who is not a reflection
but a surprise, at a thousand miles of safe
excitement? And what is it to write?
An overwhelming attention to language,

to sustain the power of precise intercourse
and still be clever. It is a working draft,
a guileless method of revision while
the Daily Self lives in the pale aura
around the letter or in the dark of the ink
still inside the pen. The letter is
a rehearsal, a listing of options,
an occasion for grace.

MAGNIFICAT

My doubt rests at the edge of a longing
for something substantial as a father,
nourishing as milk and brown bread, not
brought to clay or tears under scrutiny.
The pleasure of doubt raises my voice
like a bloom of a great blue heron,
lifts my eyes to the further vision
of an older woman reflecting my own promise.
My hands become simple dichotomies
applauding. For without doubt,
how could I resist? I could not
imagine. Would have no choice.
Being chosen is only half
the glory. Only the refrain.

NEAR THE END OF THE AFFAIR

My boots are filthy, breeches grass-stained
where I fell bum first when my mount lost
his footing, or threw me. I'm too old
to learn control of anything bigger,
more headstrong and cranky than I.

I hurt out loud and the horses slow,
fold back like time-lapse photos,
into one horse, the thoroughbred now
favoring his left front leg. We are both
sore. I get up, lead him around the arena

a few slow times to talk us into beginning
again. My foot in the stirrup, I mount
but do not lay my face against his
weed-flecked mane as I would like, to
rest as shock waves roll over, and
we hear ourselves called from the ring.

THE LOOK OF THINGS

The landscape's gotten away from me.
I let it go, single now and yard-weary.
The gardener has an eye for composition
year round. I recognize seasons
though dare not anticipate them by design.
I push my mower, clap the trimmers
like resolute applause, ease the dead
rose canes from their leafy knots.
Always I'm thinking I'm somewhere else,
that I'm only doing this gritty-itch work
for that great American title:
The Good Neighbor. I am not

a Good Neighbor. I never take soup to the sick.
If they can't open a can for themselves,
they're too sick to be at home.
I don't invite them in for coffee
because I'm at work or driving my Brownies
or hiding from people and their waving obligations.
I do smile; sometimes even from the porch swing
I'll yell across the street
at Louise who is fifty, remarried, and roller skating
figure-eights in her drive.

When I cut down that maple diseased at the trunk,
I was sad to look where it had been,
saw it still in the phantom symmetry
for a long, too long time. Now,
the grass has grown over the scar.
But when I mow, I feel the old slope.
I am careful to keep it looking smooth
to the superficial judgments of passersby.

ARBOR VITAE

The landscaper's truck cruises my block.
A second bringing bearded men
in jeans and hooded sweatshirts
stops at my dead elm.

Traveling monks, silent, deferential
to a day-glow vested boss,
have come like pilgrims to my yard.
In my house, I smile, afraid.

They are so handsome and focused,
hips buckled in tool belts, thick
saw holsters, ropes that end in hooks.
A man, thirty feet from the ground,

strokes with boots and woolen socks
the branch he must depend upon as
it shudders at the drop of proximate limbs.
So let Blake's tree blaze with angels;
mine is Darwin's vision.

From my kitchen window I see
what's left of the cockeyed family tree:
rope-tailed men tied and gauging the pitch,
guiding the fantastic rest of the fall.

WORKING CLASS GIRL MAKES GOOD

I have friends with woodburning stoves,
fireplaces swept for winter, and ricks of wood
on their decks. I will ask the city
woodcutters to saw my dead elm
into usable lengths. The slow one says
I have to ask the foreman.
Full of purpose, I mistake, perhaps,
a much handsomer man for the boss
who easily grants my request.
Then my yard is strewn with gifts
of friendly wood. Pleased with myself,
my generous forethought,
I glance out the window as
a rattly pick-up and trailer arrive,
its hand-lettered sign: Ed's Firewood Cheap.
A man and his boy talk with the foreman.
The boy's face falls; the father's jaw sets;
the woodcutter shrugs, flipping his gloves
toward my house, toward me. The trucks pull away,
all those men leaving me, my wood stacked
for burning, my clean stump, the carelessness
of a woman too long out of her class.

TIME AND MOTION

These two hands wield a trowel,
rectify the basement walls
with latex-based cement, stuff cans and papers,
the trash of an old marriage, into the cracks
that lead to earth, that slick and sticky
clay they call here gumbo,
its inexorable press against stability and space.
The whole foundation is moving out
from under the green frame house we bought
when we were thrust of a sudden into middle class
taxes and with them a baby, a fence, a shrub.
You live in an apartment and I curse you
for leaving me this basement work,
but lightly for I will take a vacation
and rent this place to a California couple
who'll leave it loopy with cat hair and cartoons
on the front and back doors, meaning welcome,
changed. There'll be new perennials in the garden.
When I return from a year away,
this home will have settled
or shifted far enough
to welcome me at least half way.

TWO POETS IN THE FAMILY

Eight hundred miles apart
we write together at 5 a.m.
What familiar theft occurs
(a blouse? a perfect brooch?) when
the gene pools so much alike arise
at the same hour in the same time zone
to make art of their lives? Who of us will
take our father this morning? Our soldier
brother dead, then a middle sister?
Which wants the tone bereft today?
Which the singular successes of our siblings
in their mystery worlds of medicine and merchandise?
Who shall damn or thank the pope
for this variety, rich and natural
resource—our mother, tired of the literal
enforcement of religion's metaphors?

It's November, Thanksgiving, nearly Advent, sister.
You live again in the family home
to which we all return—pilgrims
on our knees through the neighborhood gone
so borderline our parents can't afford to leave.
They live with us for the holidays: new cities,
new tapwater, a puzzle of sidewalks or none.
Our ends are opposite: they travel to find
the uncharted. We go to them to see again
what has already happened.

On this early train, knee sways
against careless knee. We sit across
from one another, looking out
the same window at the still dark sky;
within, the lights are rising
till we see the pane fill with reflections
of ourselves, our coming and going,
them and us, you and me.

WALKING MY BABY BACK HOME

Good Friday the church has to get rid of Jesus.
The world is bereft. We consume all our hosts.
The priest gives me two; I pocket one, a dying
god's last wish. Or an ex-nun's chance
to show him around. On the walk home, I frame him
loosely in my palm, flash him at things any one
of my friends might enjoy after long convalescence or
a sudden release from a job.

Here's a familiar sycamore tree. This is called a bike.
Three families live in that house; they are not related at all.
One family lives in this one. Yes, I know they could
shelter some homeless. (If you prick my conscience,
I'll eat you.) The driveway ahead is ours.
Come in. Do you recognize yourself here?
Three glow-in-the-dark Baby
You's afloat in holy water. The desk where I think
about nothing or us will be where you stay
propped against an amethyst—purple, liturgically apt.

I'm sure he's glad to be with me,
so I doze on the sheepskin floor.
When I awake around suppertime
and he's still helpless there,
I come to consider the scandal,
prolonging this last afternoon of his life.
We both know I can't keep him here,
can't save him from dislocation.
Though my ceiling is cracked,
no voice edges through with new rubrics.
I am left with God- or mother-wit
and take him as I would a friend
to rest beyond my lips in a dark place
where death is another word for union.

CONVENT RADIO DURING STORM SEASON

Turbulence among the veils, weather for nuns
is a pleasure. The chalice, the monstrance, the
rattling stained glass, guttering candles,
the Holy Spirit, that banshee bearing gifts,
fruits, arrives in the tail spin. We hug
the cellar walls, the frantic radio switches
mobile units, reporters not lying face down
in the ditch God gave them, snug as birth
where of course you couldn't breathe and
your whole body squirmed out of shape,
your very skull being crushed by your own
watery home contracting like blazes and
the basement crowded with virgins singing
the *Nunc Dimittis* or the *De Profundis*
Clamavi ad Te, Domine, even though the holiest
among us, the real visionary, the fat gardener,
knows full well that our Spouse, Creator of
Galaxies, loves this weather, the very fellow
who said *Lest ye become like little children*
is the hooligan whipping this up. This
is the way of the Spirit, this is the fox
in the henhouse. The man's voice, filled
with frenzy and rain, gives us his eyes
as the storm lays our landscape,
reporting the colors in faltering light
as his own grows dim and
failing, goes out. We are left alone
with hearts pumping, our good machinery,
bodies electric—not knowing whether
we've been struck by lightning or by love.

THE ESCHATOLOGICAL WARDROBE

She wears red on the feastday of a martyr,
will eat meat at every meal, until a full-bodied
wildness overtakes her. Some say she's asking
for martyrdom herself—too loud, vulgar,
calls in sick and goes shopping.

She knows what makes a martyr: an unself-
conscious, generous tease, so fleshed
even her aura is dimpled and moist.
Martyrs believe that death's been overcome,

that this now—*Take! Eat!*—is life's abundance,
so she drives home fast and there meets God
in the kitchen, sipping coffee, scrambling
a late breakfast, hair still damp from a shower,
wearing her mail order monogrammed robe.

Anyone might who makes the choice
to buy instead of turning down, distracted,
the corner of the page.

CUSTOM-PAINTED SHOES

I march in my floral feet,
sweet illusion of petal and
root. Right! Left!
Spring. These are pilgrim's
shoes: Eden to garden to grace.
These shoes draw music into
my feet, songs of plum and papaya,
drum, and the fish-leaping flash
of sopranos. These are the shoes
of the gessoed mind at attention,
the rub of correctives, one still
white rabbit near the arch.
Oh, the adjustable fit!
Even under my bed, they hum
a little tune just for being
just for me.

TRANSLATION OF LIGHTS

for my sister, the artist (1951–1973)

When I lived above the lavender
in the mountains of Southern France
I wished you there; such night skies
filled with van Gogh. To the crown
of his broad-brimmed hat he fastened
candles, propped his easel in a sweet bouquet,
a field on a night like this
crazed with stars,
whose wheeling and pulsing,
whose very light left them, it must have been
thousands, oh thousands of years ago.

NOON: THE BALANCING HOUR

Bastille Day, 1992

The bell rings over Île St Honorat
a single toll to call the monks from fields
of lavender and thyme, from apiaries
full-combed and dripping,
to wash and robe for prayer at 12:15.
The chapel nave fills with tourists
come to celebrate
all overthrown oppression, here. Ironic
place to do it, an abbey on an island.
To picnic on the grounds, to purchase
audiocassettes of chanted Office, packets
of herbs, postcards, honey, Cistercian liqueurs.
I buy an olivewood cross, its grain like
sweeping long hair. "Made by a hermit,"
the cashier monk says, and I who am feeling
especially alone, the condition of my secular
humanity, this day think, "What is not?"
and follow the second bell to chapel.

I have lived this life myself
years back and made my way here, to spend
the day before vacation's end. My daughter
Margaret across the harbor on Île Ste Marguerite
lies barebreasted on the beach,
the last chance, her long unruly hair pulled
back tight from habit and desire not to mar
such an expanse of tan. She to her name's island,
I to rebuilt ruins—each true to her own.

The cantor on the Gospel side chants the antiphon
and as we sing back the response, he licks a knuckle
firmly where the honey must've stuck. O taste
and see! I remember that. And vexing distraction

when all you want is the wholehearted flow.
Margaret had a boyfriend wholly self-absorbed who
whined the worst of being a busboy was that
honey for the rolls seemed to travel during dinner
over salt shakers, ashtrays, chairbacks. When
they broke up, she paid a friend to sweeten his tables.

Halfway around this world and the next,
at the closing of Office,
the monks by twos genuflect, make
their Profound Inclinations, and process
to the refectory, to stoneware bowls of black
bean soup, baguettes and cheese, the garlicky
odor of sanctity. Over baskets of fruit,
their desserts a humming nimbus, the bees
still unsatisfied are waved off, out the leaded
watery windows to where the monks will be
once they return to their cells, hang those voluminous
habits on doorpegs, and meet at the shed for shovels
and hoes, the compost forks that turn waste
back to dirt, the sweet yoke that connects
and in that connecting makes us free.

WORLD ENOUGH

Before harsh angles of logic or speech,
in the marveling quiet of morning,
a woman spills over color and curve
like an antelope
frilling the arc of the earth, leaping
body bent to the shape of grace,
then gone into a deep forest
where God, surprised,
blooms like a white peacock.

WONDER BREAD

"Hocus pocus": corruption of
"Hoc est enim corpus meum"

One April day the mad priest
approached a bakery truck and prayed
the words of consecration. The driver,
a parishioner, called the bishop to buy
every biscuit, loaf and bun; the whole
cargo the Body of Christ.
If that priest is still loose
changing substantially everything
he knows he knows how,

what if no one overhears? Kids will
eat those sweetrolls and stop
their breakfast fight; a man slipping
the sandwich from his sack will find
his union dues; the student
over midnight toast sees life and major
work; imagine the flap and chatter aloft,
full of breadcrumbs, the birds.

The Hermit Woman

A WAY

Something dark and rough
leads into that life.
It is quiet like fear
or a final confrontation,
solitude: the walnut
resting under its own tree
offering itself
to something hungry.

GROUNDING

Dots of thorn fires snap and blaze
at every level of the quarry. Sparks
drift around prayers and disappear
in the dark chill of this desert
in its third century of waiting
for a Second Coming, a last chance.
These fires are the nightly irregularities
that quicken the quarry's pulse.
In praise or fury, they fling
thin shadows reeling
against limestone.

Between her fire and her cave
the woman stands, arms wide as wings,
her black hair a shaggy cape.
She chants into the quarry as the earth
rolls it under the moon.

An ostrich and her sleeping young
rustle inside their own prayer;
a young man in a nearby cave
sighs under dream breasts.
Night sounds flicker like memories
of pleasure in very old age.

In this world, in her way
the woman chants every night
for the restoration of holiness
and the palpable need for it.

GRANDMOTHER GOD

You delivered land out of water, settled
radiant horizons with variety, then the need
for legs. That was when you knew time flash,
the glint of something turning perhaps away.

With evolution's ears like petals and shells,
you listen now for your early comfort,
the voice you found for necessity.

Although the dark has thinned, gone
vague with shadows, is not what
you would recall; though even your name
is quiet, you are aware of that old hum,
dissatisfaction rising again like a resource.

LYING-IN

There is a high correlation between
being filled with the Spirit and
being filled with the Flesh.

Sleep carries her through the wall
to a further cave, darker, inaccessible
except through bathing, through fasting,
through rituals of introversion.

She turns on her mat.
This is a heavy comfort,
this kind of privacy.

She is filling with a new life, not hers,
a life that belongs to itself, a flight,
a dive, a suspension. It pushes her out
through her own skin, manufacturing distance
in its helpless excitement.

THE NAME OF GOD IS

simple as the attraction
of nipple and mouth;
the spring songs
of everything seasonal.
Expansive as bread.
Creatures of a silent life
store it outside the interruption
of syllables (as mountain, desert,
deepest water). Beasts are born
with it hidden like an extra cord
in the voicebox. The name of God
is a great cave in which
we say our own names and
our own names return to us
round as song; full of snow;
striking.

INSIDE, THE LANDSCAPE

The way to ascend to God
is to descend into oneself.

If I shut my eyes I can see
inside my mouth: lagoon, cliffs, three
tied boats. There are too many.
I move down past harps hung on willows,
down past the park of green feathers,
bushes full, humid. And still
farther to the split
of sand. I am getting there:
shimmers of heat and the smell
of honey and lions. I am somewhere
close to my knees.

CONVERSATION WITH GOD

When I say my name, I am telling you
a story. I am giving you a song
singing. Singing in the crossroads,
at the intersection of planes,
in affection's impossible geometry:
reversing; angling; curling; tangential;
my own name circumscribing another's
while it is itself embraced, bound.

It is the story of bursting luggage,
a hole in the road, late night noises
in your neighborhood. It is the story
of good teeth, light around the corner,
seven fountains, a reserve of energy.

Inside my name, time collapses.
This too is the story. My name is
another language, not reasonable,
not hormonal, trusting. It blesses
as it moves toward your own.

AS IN ICONS

Three barefoot travelers, chinless,
restrained, carrying red wands,
short knives, a wallet of cheese
or bread, offer news
for an iron key.

She says this is the desert.
They say perhaps the garden or well
has keys buried in its walls
by someone who left too many children
or creditors back in the city years ago
to come here to pray not to be found,
to divest her belt of their weight,
of their traceable jangle.

She says in the desert caves have locks
of language or of bones sharpened
to the language of denial.
She says this is a riddle:
I am a question

or I am an answer

or, amused, I am an imagination
of your flesh.

She vanishes in a ripple of heat.

They walk full-faced,
both feet pointing east,
eyes two dimensional.

CORRESPONDENCE

Letters arrive and are stored
under a rock in her cell.
She saves them for feast days.

The entire cell is blackened
on those days, scorched clay
halfway up. She dresses
in the old garb, fries the morning.

Hunger makes bowls of her eyes
to catch spangles, a drizzle
of black dots, and halos.
A shimmering napkin lifts
and falls over the doorway.

Now the food throws itself
to the animals, the letters
slip from under their rock
and burrow into sand
miles deep. She settles
into the rest between holidays.

THE TEMPTATION TO PRIDE

This woman lives in comfort.
Where are the hermits, she asks.
Where are those gritty-eyed eunuchs
who slip around stone like water
or wind, demanding from me
a reason for their god?

They are held like the owl
by day, by the vexations
of light, the white hum
of the noonday devil.
In their cells they count
ibex, date pits, prayers.
Longing for holy conversation,
they gaze here and there
for a visitor, sighing
in confusion until finally
the day rolls away
behind the mountains
weary of such vacancy.

WHAT THE WOMAN MUTTERS
AT THE MOUTH OF HER CAVE

And why I wait now standing
all night, palms up, burning slow
as hide, I cannot say. Except perhaps
in hope of exchange,
in hope of getting back.

I expect my due, and more: blood and milk
and sweet sweet honey, the grace
not to have to share with the broken
animals, my brothers and sisters,
mother and father, all poor relations.

I have surprised you with gifts:
my teeth; the long refreshment of bathing
after dark; conversation in bed
with a handsome, clean man.

And now I want only
what I gave, that promise.
I want to survive
one overwhelming satisfaction.

TWO STEPS FORWARD

Down to the well
the woman carries her vessel
carved with animal shapes
rampant, huddled,
astir with a memory vague
as bees around a dead log,
a blurred hum of
how it was before the human
animal stood upright, singular,
absent minded. Further back
of how they all were once
water creatures: splashing woman
and splashing lion in a cold flip
of scales and flat eyes,
that phantom strangeness of no legs
or paws when this desert
earth was thick with seaweed
ripe and breathless. Now the woman
hairy and dry, their distant sister,
returns to water, returns them all
to water.

VOCATION

She cannot recall how she got there,
her memory, an exhalation.

She swirls three shells,
lifts one: unfettered, a nest
empty above a fanged portcullis.

Lifts another: olive merchant,
snake in a basket, jasmine.

The third: a body of water
liberal as a harlot's mirror.

However it was she arrived,
it was nothing so simple
as one tangible pea under a shell.

SOMETHING THE WOMAN DREAMS

Birds never light on my walls,
my hanging columns; in old age
my air is hingeless, steady,
quiet as down against stone
or water. A river slides
through me to my daughter.

In her the birds and I can
sleep, silver wings covering
our heads, talons locked
in the limbs of shaggy trees.
A forest breathes like mist,
she tells me. The water pulls
itself up inside trees near dawn;
she bears her children
through their own dream air
into birds, back into me.

VISITORS AND THEIR VARIOUS EVIDENCE

God wears a shirt of poppies,
comes to her, spread as a sunset,
substantial. He enters her cave
touching the candles
hung near the door, the water jug
shaped like a torso. He will not
touch her and there is that
determination, that conditioned
ache to be desirable
and indifferent.

The rush of his departure is relief.
A young ibex peeks in, steps gingerly
toward her basket of herbs. Brushing
his forehead against her knee, he waits
to be fed though there are petals
everywhere. He will get them
when she sweeps.

RUMINATION

The silence offers her direction:
a breeze brushes rock, basil
in the doorway cracks its brown pockets,
fibers of her wooden bowl close over
sand. The woman stands near her mat,
hair tied to a hook in the ceiling
for wakefulness, living out loud
with the wood and the herbs.

GIFTS OF THE SPIRIT

When too much sun burns her salty,
her thoughts turn to other spices,
seafaring men bearing gifts—
cinnamon, saffron, ginger.

A red-eyed mare spurred by heat and memory,
she gallops over her own edge to the cold sea
she remembers miles below.
On impact she shatters, splashing all over
herself, like sunrise.

SHAPING THE PAST

began with the need for a berth,
a place to sleep off the earth,
a ledge or shelf in her cell, a bed
in old age—another of God's gifts

she'd like to give back. What began
with a scoop in the cave became sculpture,
the graven image of herself as
herself before God, older than God,

in the oldest profession. First, a foot.
She scraped away what wasn't her foot,
but the ankle bracelet or a seam
in the earth remained. Playful, work

around me, it said. Up her calves,
the great vise thighs, the stone warming
as her past lay back. At last,
the hermit received her, odalisque

arms open, breast a banquette. And,
ah! the hair. Gardens, lush earthy curls
and extensions, the business of business.
When God had requested her lavish

investment, the grand expenditure, she'd
wedged herself into this purse in the wall,
her past a jingle of bangles and earrings,
coins of the realm, o Beloved, small change.

MERCY

Morning renews her temptation
to be pleased by predictable day,
to depend on its easy continuity.
Fill the jar with water
for steeping new palm leaves;
trade beans for wheat at the well;
weave baskets for market.
The buzz of gentle commerce thins
at dusk and simple connections
let go.

Gazelle and lion shudder
in each other's dreams;
hyena and sheep are at rest.
What remains is unexpected,
is irrational: all night the woman
in her closed cell chanting.
Beyond her door is the desert;
at the edge of the desert
are the villages, then port cities,
and the sea bound by the ends
of the earth, all of which ring
one woman at prayer.

ACKNOWLEDGMENTS

Thanks to the editors of the following publications. Some of the poems appeared in earlier versions.

AMERICA: "The Turning Point"
THE BELLINGHAM REVIEW: "The Self as Linear with a Bell at the End," "World Without End"
BELOIT POETRY JOURNAL: "Preparing the Way"
CAROLINA QUARTERLY: "World Enough"
CHICAGO REVIEW: "Correspondence" (formerly "Letters Arrive"), "Inside the Landscape" (formerly "If I shut my eyes")
THE COLORADO QUARTERLY: "Methods of Organization"
THE GEORGIA REVIEW: "In Random Fields of Impulse and Repose," "The Name of God Is"
THE GREENSBORO REVIEW: "Misperceptions," "An Urban Cosmology," "Translation of Lights"
IMAGE: "Left Hand Is Complement," "Noon: The Balancing Hour," "Wonder Bread," "Walking My Baby Back Home"
KANSAS QUARTERLY: (from *The Hermit Woman*) "A Way," "Vocation" (formerly "Shell Game"), "Lying-In" (formerly "Sleep carries her"), "As in Icons," "Grounding," "The Temptation to Pride," "Mercy," "Rumination"; also, "Magnificat," "Like A Jaguar" (formerly "Counsel"), "Sinister," "Fido," "Arbor Vitae"
MIDWEST POETRY REVIEW: "The Self as Constellation," "Visitors and Their Various Evidence"
MIKROKOSMOS: "Looking Both Ways"
NEW ORLEANS REVIEW: "Conversation with God"
NORTHEAST: "Reconnaissance," "Something the Woman Dreams," "Mercy as the Constant," "Death and Tracking"
NORTHERN LIT. QUARTERLY: "Time and Motion"
THE OHIO REVIEW: "Sometimes the Coming of Babies," "Difference in Ages," "Poem for Christmas"
POETRY NORTHWEST: "What the Woman Mutters at the Mouth of Her Cave"
RIVER STYX: "When the Bough Breaks," "Two Poets in the Family"
SHOCKER: "The Look of Things"
THE SMITH: "After Separation," "Gifts of the Spirit"
WOMAN-POET: "Grandmother God," "Two Steps Forward"

"The Left Hand Is Complement" appears in THE BEST SPIRITUAL WRITING 2000 (HarperSanFrancisco).
"The Name of God Is" appears in KEENER SOUNDS: SELECTED POEMS FROM *The Georgia Review*, 1987.
"In Random Fields of Impulse and Repose" appears in ANTHOLOGY OF MAGAZINE VERSE AND YEARBOOK OF AMERICAN POETRY: 1981.
"World Enough" and "Conversation with God" appear in ANTHOLOGY OF MAGAZINE VERSE AND YEARBOOK OF AMERICAN POETRY: 1980.